CLASSIFIED

SECRETS YOU'RE NOT SUPPOSED TO KNOW

THE UNDERWORLD

Criminals in Action

Anita Croy

LUCENT
PRESS

Published in 2019 by
Lucent Press, an Imprint of Greenhaven Publishing, LLC
353 3rd Avenue
Suite 255
New York, NY 10010

For Brown Bear Books Ltd:
Managing Editor: Tim Cooke
Designer: Lynne Lennon
Children's Publisher: Anne O'Daly
Design Manager: Keith Davis
Editorial Director: Lindsey Lowe
Picture Manager: Sophie Mortimer

Picture Credits
t=top, c=center, b=bottom, l=left, r=right
Interior: Alamy: Paul Fearn, 27, Hemis, 18; AP: 17; Art Institute of Chicago: Mr and Mrs Lewis Larned Coburn Memorial Collection, 29; Business Insider: Mike Bird, 20; Dreamstime: Wongsalam77, 32; Getty Images: 44, AFP/Yuri Cortez, 41, John Moore, 42, NY Daily News Archive, 28, Wireimage/Rebecca Sapp, 9; iStock: Cecilie_Arcurs, 15, dicus63, 10, loca4motion, 40, PeopleImages, 32, 35, Rawpixel, 26, sprng23, 24, supershabashnyl, 4, Uncleroo, 7, zorazhuang, 39; Library of Congress: 8; Public Domain: Designofgrace.com, 1, 23, Mailguard, 34, Mariordo, 21, NHS UK, 36, Outlook, 37, parliament.uk, 18; Shutterstock: 43, Francois Boizot, 16, hkhtt hj, 25, Jordi C, 33, Udom Settawat, 11, David S. Swierczek, 13, Yuttanas, 12; US Coast Guard Service: 45; US Customs and Border Protection: 5.
Front cover: (background) Monika Gruszewicz/Shutterstock.com; (foreground) DenisProduction.com/ Shutterstock.com.

Brown Bear Books has made every attempt to contact the copyright holder.
If anyone has any information please contact licensing@brownbearbooks.co.uk

Cataloging-in-Publication Data

Names: Croy, Anita.
Title: The underworld: criminals in action / Anita Croy.
Description: New York : Lucent Press, 2019. | Series: Classified: secrets you're not supposed to know | Includes glossary and index.
Identifiers: ISBN 9781534564473 (pbk.) | ISBN 9781534564459 (library bound)
Subjects: LCSH: Organized crime--Juvenile literature. | Gangs--Juvenile literature. | Computer crimes--Juvenile literature.
Classification: LCC HV6441.C79 2019 | DDC 364.106--dc23

Manufactured in the United States of America

CPSIA Compliance Information: Batch #BS18KL
For further information contact Rosen Publishing, New York, New York at 1-800-237-9932

CONTENTS

CRIME IN THE MODERN AGE

The nature of crime is changing. The growth of the Internet has made traditional types of crime easier and has also led to new types of crime.

Most crime sets out to profit from illegal activity. For centuries, this has involved stealing, supplying fake or stolen goods, or running forbidden activities such as gambling. Criminals have used violence and threats to protect what they do. These activities still continue, as do the threats and violence. However, new types of **cybercrime** increasingly attract criminal gangs as well as individuals. They offer potentially high returns for low levels of risk.

>> Cybercrime Criminals have been quick to see the opportunities for crime created by the use of computers and the Internet.

>> **Drug Shipment** Border agents display packages of drugs hidden in a truck brought into the United States.

FIGHTING CRIME

The fight against crime is also fought with new technology. While **hackers** try to steal people's passwords and security data online, banks and online retailers are investing large sums of money to protect their customers. Drug dealers are using **satellite** technology to smuggle drugs into the United States. But law enforcement agencies are using satellite photography to disrupt the drug dealers' operations. Criminals use part of the Internet known as the **Dark Web** to sell stolen goods and other illegal items. Meanwhile, police forces hire their own computer experts to try to follow **illicit** payments or trace the holders of illegal bank accounts.

ORGANIZED CRIME

Criminal gangs control an illegal global business that is bigger than the national economy of Spain. Organized crime is worth around $900 billion a year.

Organized crime gangs operate across the world. Some are relatively small, but others are so large they have become **notorious**. They include, for example, the Mafia and the Hells Angels in the United States, the Yakuza in Japan, the triads in China, and the Russian Bratva. Such gangs are behind a large proportion of serious crime, including "traditional" crimes—such as selling illegal drugs, **trafficking** people, and controlling illegal gambling—and cybercrime, such as committing online **identity theft** and **fraud**. Today, organized crime affects almost everyone.

Organized crime is based on close-knit groups who swear **loyalty** to each other. The Mafia had its own code of honor based on loyalty to the organization, which acted as a kind of family. Many criminal gangs were run by real families. The Kray twins ran a gang in London, England, in the 1960s.

>> Hells Angels Police say the gang is involved in organized crime in the United States. The Hells Angels say they are just a group of bikers.

FAST FACTS

CRIMINAL GANGS

Organized crime is the name given to criminal acts carried out by gangs. Some gangs are small and operate on a local scale. Others are huge organizations with hundreds of members and helpers. They have the power and influence to gain the support of **corrupt** officials.

THE MAFIA

Large-scale organized crime in the United States is about 100 years old. It started in the 1920s, during Prohibition, which banned the sale of alcoholic drinks. The ban soon led to an illegal market in selling liquor. The trade was controlled by recently arrived Italian immigrants. Italy had a history of criminal gangs in regions such as the island of Sicily. The gangs that emerged in the United States used the same methods as the Italian gangs: violence and threats. The American gangsters used violence to control their interests in cities such as New York and Chicago.

>> Prohibition Federal agents pour illegal liquor down a drain during a police raid.

FOR AND AGAINST

The U.S. government often relies on criminals for information. Criminals who secretly give information to police are known as informers. In the 1980s, a member of the Mafia named Henry Hill gave information to the authorities to avoid going to prison. His information led to the convictions of 50 other mobsters. Hill's life later inspired the movie *Goodfellas*. Should criminals who help the authorities be pardoned? Or should they still be punished for their crimes?

>> Goodfellas Henry Hill (left) was played in the movie by Ray Liotta (right).

They set up syndicates, or associations, in which crime "families" agreed to cooperate and not to compete with each other. When gangs did fight over territory, there was often violence. On Valentine's Day, February 14, 1929, mobsters in Chicago shot dead seven members of another gang.

WORLDWIDE NETWORK

Today, organized crime is a global business. The collapse of the Soviet Union in 1991 led to a rapid growth of criminal gangs in Russia and eastern Europe. The influence of these gangs is far-reaching. U.S. intelligence agencies accused Russian crime gangs for interfering with the U.S. presidential election of 2016, for example. Some people believe the gangs operated with the support of the Russian government.

WHAT DO YOU THINK?

After the Soviet Union collapsed in 1991, a period of chaos followed. In Russia, criminals fought to control the country's **assets.** Since then, the Russian government of Vladimir Putin (above, in red tie) has been closely linked to criminal gangs. Some experts claim that Russia is a criminal state. They point to its corrupt officials and its interference in other governments' business. The government is also said to have been involved in the murder of Russian citizens such as Alexander Litvinenko, who was poisoned in the UK. If Russia is a criminal state, should other countries still work with it?

TYPES OF CRIME

Organized crime operates at every level of daily life. Its primary purpose is to make the most money for the least effort. This is why the criminals are attracted to illegal activity such as drugs, where the profit margins are high. While money is the main motivation for organized crime, some criminals also like the power that goes with **bribing** and **blackmailing** others.

Organized criminals use the latest technology to steal money from organizations and individuals. They are often responsible for large-scale Internet security breaches in which personal data is stolen. Crime gangs include computer experts who can hack into any system anywhere in the world. The gangs also control **counterfeiters**, who produce fake versions of currency and valuable goods. They make fake paintings, wine, luxury handbags and watches, electrical goods, pirated movies, and medicines.

>> **Counterfeit** Fake designer handbags on sale at a market in Bangkok, Thailand.

Organized crime is also behind a large proportion of car theft in Europe, in which luxury vehicles are stolen to order. The gangs employ criminals who have figured out how to clone electronic car fobs. They can take a car and transport it far away before the owner even realizes it is missing.

ONLINE MARKETPLACE

The rise of the Internet has created a whole new market for organized criminals to sell their fake goods. Part of the Internet called the Dark Web has become known as a place for buying and selling stolen or illegal goods. It is set up so that it is difficult for law enforcement to trace the criminals behind it. The Internet also provides criminal gangs with other new forms of business. In addition to stealing identities, criminal gangs distribute **malware** that locks people's computers and demands a **ransom** to unlock them.

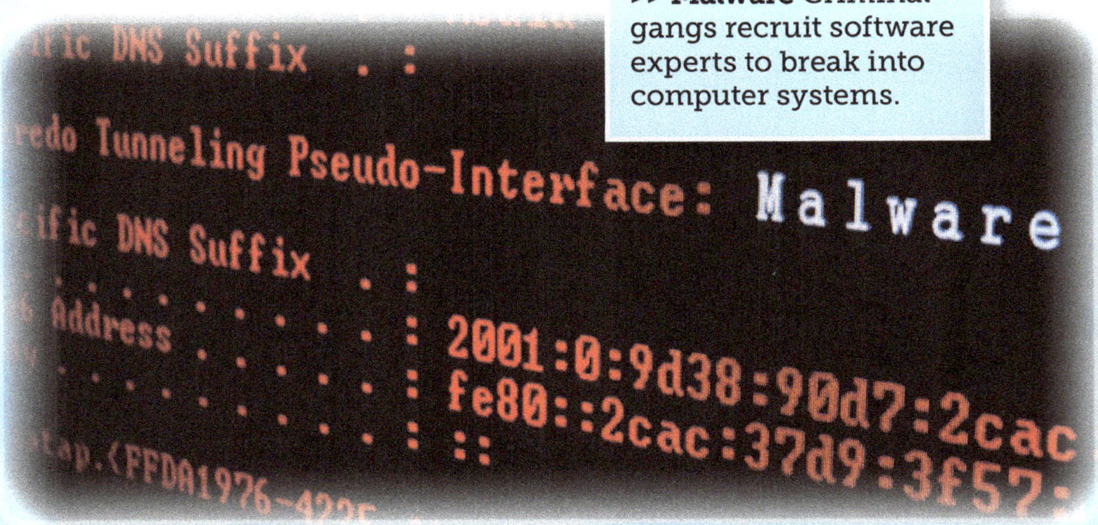

>> **Malware** Criminal gangs recruit software experts to break into computer systems.

MALWARE

Malware is the name given to malicious computer software used by criminal gangs to access computer systems. Malware comes in different forms, including **viruses** and worms that damage computers, spyware that tracks users' activity, and "Trojan horses" that can take control of whole networks of linked computers.

TAX EVASION

A common element of criminal activity is that gangs pay no taxes. They have elaborate financial operations to keep the vast sums they earn under the radar of the Internal Revenue Service (IRS) and other tax authorities around the world. Some gangs are run as sophisticated businesses. They hide their money in the same ways as legitimate businesses do, by setting up **offshore** companies, for example.

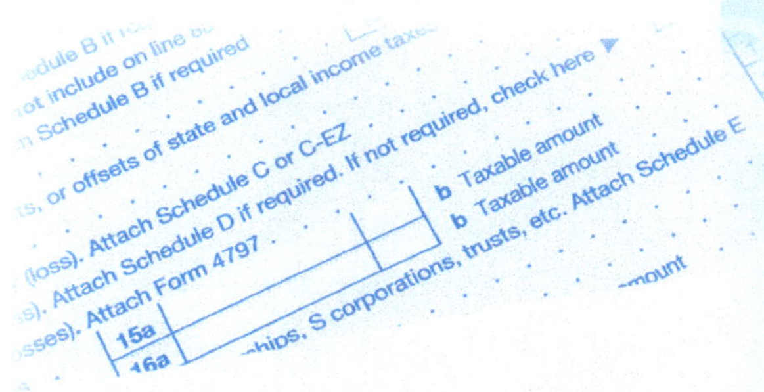

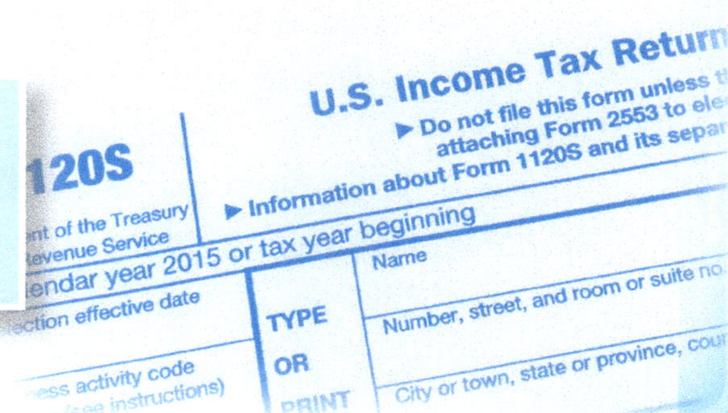

>> Tax Evasion Criminal gangs go to great lengths to avoid paying tax on their income.

CORRUPTION

Corruption exists on different levels. Sometimes it operates as people offering a small tip to a local official in return for a favor. At others, it is a multimillion dollar crime against a whole country.

Corruption is widely understood as dishonest behavior by people in power, usually in return for a bribe or other financial gain. However, in practice, corruption can be harder to define. In some countries, politicians steal money from public funds for their own use. This seems an obvious example of corruption, but the politicians might claim that they need the money to entertain visitors from overseas. In other places, a local official might give someone access to a politician in return for a small payment. But the official might claim that the money was just a gift, not a bribe, and did not influence their decision.

Some people use connections to try to gain advantages for their families or their friends. Members of groups such as the Freemasons or elk lodges may recommend fellow members for jobs. A parent might use their influence to gain an internship for a child, or perhaps find employment for their children or other relatives in their own place of work.

>> Handshake
If a person makes a business deal with someone who is also a friend, is that an example of corruption?

FAST FACTS

GRAND AND PETTY

Legal definitions distinguish between grand and petty corruption. Grand corruption involves people at high levels of government and business. Petty corruption is on a much lower level. It usually concerns minor officials who receive tips and gifts.

GRAND CORRUPTION

In legal terms, grand corruption is a crime in which rulers or governments make decisions not in the general interest but in the interests of themselves or their supporters. In 2017, for example, a French court found Teodoro Obiang, son of the president of Equatorial Guinea in Africa, guilty of acquiring his wealth through corruption. Obiang held a ministerial role paying $80,000 a year, but he had a lavish lifestyle that could not be afforded on such a salary, including a huge mansion in Paris. Obiang was accused of taking bribes in return for selling off Equatorial Guinea's timber resources.

>> **Avenue Foch** Teodoro Obiang owned a 101-room house on this expensive street in Paris. The house was valued at 107 million euros.

Every year since 1993, the organization Transparency International has published a list of the most and least corrupt countries in the world.

Five most corrupt countries in 2017:	Five least corrupt countries in 2017:
1. Somalia	1. New Zealand
2. South Sudan	2. Denmark
3. Syria	3. Finland
4. Afghanistan	4. Norway
5. Yemen	5. Switzerland

TOP SECRET

Grand corruption is often associated with undeveloped or developing countries. Equatorial Guinea, for example, is a poor country with low **life expectancy**. Grand corruption is also common in countries suffering from war or with failed governments.

>> **War-torn** Corruption is highest in Somalia, which has been devastated by conflict.

PETTY CORRUPTION

In contrast to grand corruption, petty corruption takes place every day all over the world. To many people, it might be defined as doing a favor for a friend or being given a small reward or gift for helping somebody if you are in any position of power.

>> **Freemasons** Some people see the way in which members of clubs and organizations help one another as a form of corruption.

In parts of the Middle East and South Asia, for example, it is common to hear the word *baksheesh*. Beggars use it to ask for money, and it can mean a tip for a service. It is also refers to bribing a person to get something that would not be available otherwise. This can vary from something minor, such as getting a good table in a restaurant, to jumping the line to see an important government official.

POLITICAL CORRUPTION

Corruption is not only a problem in the developing world. Western democracies are also associated with corruption. This might take the shape of using influence to award government contracts to friends and allies, or an official leaving public office to take a job in part of the **private sector** they were previously responsible for regulating. Politicians might also use public office to gain financial advantage.

WHAT DO YOU THINK?

When U.S. presidents take office they traditionally put their business interests into a **blind trust.** This means they take no part in any financial activity, so they cannot profit from being president. In 2017, President Donald Trump refused to use a blind trust. Instead, he transferred his businesses to his sons to oversee. Do you think that is enough of a separation between his presidency and his business interests?

In the UK, a political scandal broke out in 2009. A newspaper investigation revealed that many members of parliament (MPs) had been claiming expenses to which they were not entitled. They claimed for second homes in London that they then rented out at a profit. Some claimed for items that were unrelated to their political job. One MP submitted a claim for a floating house for ducks on his garden pond.

>> **Parliament** A scandal broke out when it became clear British politicians were taking advantage of generous expense allowances.

THE COSTS OF CORRUPTION

Corruption has various costs. Political corruption interferes with the democratic process and the rule of law. Economic corruption removes valuable resources from the economy. In Russia, for example, President Vladimir Putin's family and close associates have amassed fortunes in a country where the average salary is around $500 a month. When money is taken from government funds like this, schools and hospitals do not get built. On a social level, corruption makes people suspicious. They may begin to mistrust each other and the political organizations that control their country.

>> Privilege
A young intern works in a bank. Such placements are highly sought after and hard to get without help.

WHAT DO YOU THINK?

Imagine you want a summer internship in a law firm to put on your resumé. A family friend works in that firm and says they will put in a good word for you. Some people say that is simply helping out a friend. Others say it is corrupt because the lawyer is abusing a position of power. Is this fair?

ENVIRONMENTAL CORRUPTION

One potentially life-threatening form of corruption is environmental corruption. In 2015, for example, it was discovered that the German auto company, Volkswagen, had been illegally fixing the results of tests to measure emissions from its diesel vehicles. The results made the cars appear better for the environment than they really were. The scandal engulfed almost every automobile manufacturer when it was discovered that many companies had been fixing their emissions test. The impact of the illicit toxic emissions on people's health and the environment is yet to be fully figured out.

>> False Claim Volkswagen's claim that its Golf model was environmentally friendly was based on fixed test results.

FRAUD

There are many words for a fraud, such as scam, swindle, extortion, sham, hoax, or confidence trick. Whatever it is called, fraud has one aim: to make money illegally.

The aim of a fraud is to trick a person or business out of money or other property. There are two broad categories. In the first, consumers buy goods or services for which they either do not pay or pay using money that they have stolen. In the second, suppliers sell consumers goods that are not what they claim to be or services that do not exist.

Fraud has existed for thousands of years. For example, almost all ancient societies had severe punishments to prevent people from producing fake coins that did not match the same value of gold or silver as official coins. People caught counterfeiting coins could be put to death. Early in the 21st century, fraud was on the rise thanks to the increased use of the Internet for buying and selling goods and for online banking. Fraudsters use the **anonymity** of the web to gain illegal access to people's identities and bank accounts. They use this information to steal money or to buy goods or services at someone else's expense. However, this is only one type of fraud that has been made easier by the rise of new technology.

FAST FACTS

COUNTERFEITING

The counterfeiting business, which makes fake versions of famous brands, makes up nearly 3 percent of global economic activity. Experts estimate it was worth up to $1.13 trillion in 2017.

>> Ladies Market This market in Hong Kong, China, is famous for selling counterfeit goods.

The rise of online selling sites also opened new opportunities for fraud, particularly in the selling of fake goods. Individuals on the sites buy from suppliers who are often anonymous. This means that customers have no way to complain if the items they buy turn out to be fake.

The Internet also opened new avenues for the trade in illegal goods such as drugs and firearms. Billions of spam emails around the world offer cheap medical drugs. Most people delete the emails, but if only a tiny percentage of people who receive the email order drugs, the effort is worthwhile for the criminals behind it.

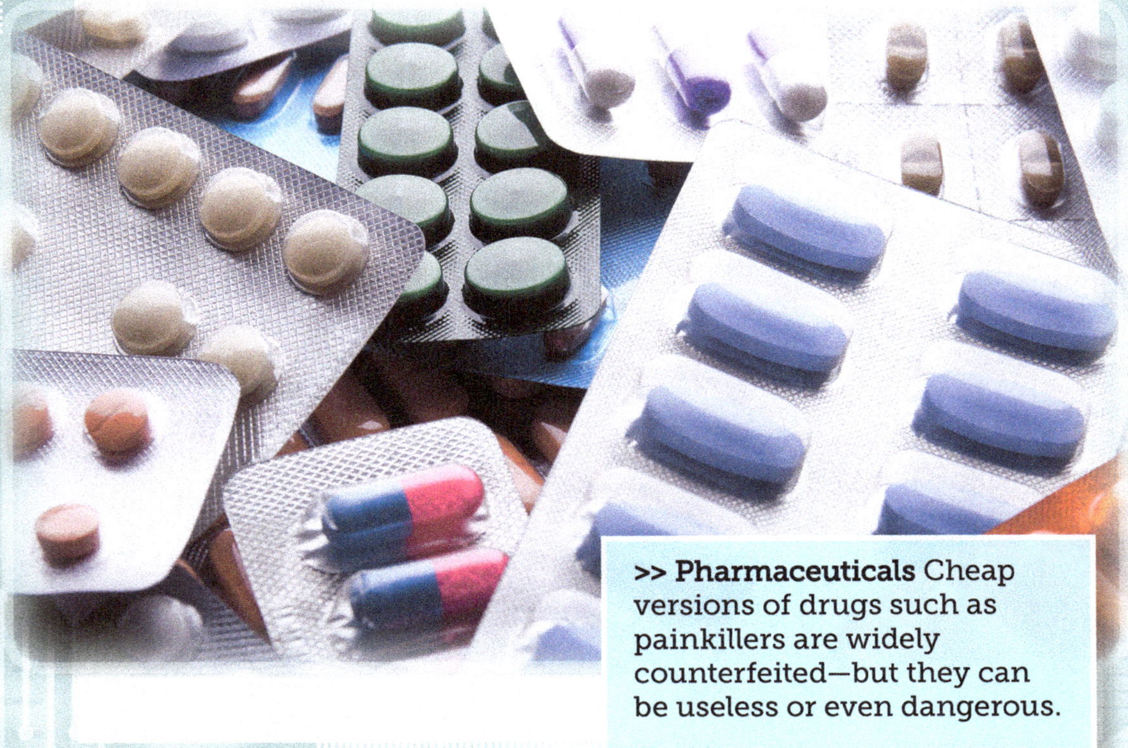

>> **Pharmaceuticals** Cheap versions of drugs such as painkillers are widely counterfeited—but they can be useless or even dangerous.

FOR AND AGAINST

Fraud is now a global business. When fraudsters are arrested, they might be in a different country from the country that is charging them with a crime. Some people say they should be tried where they are arrested. Others say the criminals will not face justice unless they are sent to the country where they are accused.

>> Wristwatch Designer watches are among the most commonly counterfeited goods.

TOO GOOD TO BE TRUE

One main area of fraud is the manufacture of counterfeit, or fake, goods. These are usually goods that appear to be genuine items, such as designer-label handbags or expensive watches, but are much cheaper copies. Other common forgeries include tickets for music or sports events, or even money. In fall 2017, the Bank of England withdrew the £1 coin from circulation because it had become too easy for criminals to counterfeit. In the late 20th century, the counterfeit trade was based in East Asia. Street markets in Thailand or Hong Kong became tourist destinations as people visited to buy fake Nike shoes or Ralph Lauren polos. The main center of counterfeiting now is China. In the city of Shenzen, for example, counterfeiters produce pirated computer hardware—sometimes as soon as the official product is released.

>> **Banking** Finance organizations such as banks have become major targets for criminals.

The Internet has provided additional outlets for fake goods. Not only do the fraudsters take money from their customers under false pretenses. They also defraud the genuine manufacturers of potential sales.

IT'S MY MONEY

The Internet has also enabled the rise of financial fraud. Criminals have developed highly sophisticated ways of stealing the details of bank accounts and credit-card users. They target individuals to try to trick them into revealing their details. Or the criminals breach security to steal details from the databases held by retailers. Stealing personal information allows criminals to carry out fraudulent activities using that stolen data.

OLD-FASHIONED SCAMS

Not all frauds rely on computers. Some financial fraud relies on the greed and **naivety** of people. One notorious type of scam is the pyramid scheme, or Ponzi scheme. It is centuries old, but that does not stop it from attracting investors.

The scheme operates on the principle of "robbing Peter to pay Paul." Someone offers investors a chance to make a large return by investing money. As more investors join, the scheme uses their money to pay returns to the earlier investors. The scheme works well until investors want to withdraw their money or people stop investing altogether. There is nothing left, and the most recent investors have lost all their money for no return.

>> Charles Ponzi
Ponzi spent five years in jail for his pyramid scheme.

PONZI SCHEMES

Ponzi schemes take their name from New York con man Charles Ponzi. In 1920, Ponzi promised investors a 40 percent return in just 90 days at a time when 5 percent was the typical return on investments. To begin with, Ponzi made a million dollars a day. However, when the scheme collapsed after only a year, it was discovered that the initial "investment" opportunity was just $30 of mail coupons!

TOP SECRET

Weather: Partly to mostly sunny, 43/31
SPORTS ★ FINAL
Friday, March 13, 2009
DAILY NEWS
2.5 MILLION READERS EVERY DAY
NYDailyNews.com
50¢
61727-054
BERNIE MADOFF IN SLAMMER AT LAST - PAGES 4-8
Why take a chance? Play both!
$26 Million! $23 Million!
NEW YORK LOTTO

>> In Jail Bernie Madoff ran one of the most powerful companies on Wall Street—but its success was a sham.

The most famous Ponzi scheme of recent times was the biggest ever seen. In 2009, New York financier Bernie Madoff was jailed for 150 years. His financial company had run a huge Ponzi scheme that stole $64.8 billion from its investors.

FAKE ART

One element in the rise of modern fraud has been the appearance of a new, wealthy consumer. From the late decades of the 20th century, the growth of **capitalism** in China and Russia created many new billionaires. One way they showed their wealth was by buying art. That encouraged fakers to produce counterfeit art. In the Dafen suburb of Shenzen in China, for example, is an "oil-painting village." Thousands of artists there produce fake versions of famous paintings. Some experts now claim that half the works available in the art market are fake. In 2016, the famous auction house Sotheby's was caught out when a 16th-century Dutch painting it sold to a U.S. buyer for $10.6 million was found to be a fake.

>> Two Sisters
French artist Pierre-Auguste Renoir painted *Two Sisters* in Paris in 1881.

REAL OR FAKE

In October 2017, President Donald Trump became caught up in an argument about whether a painting he owned is real or a fake. Pierre-Auguste Renoir's *Two Sisters* has belonged to the Chicago Institute of Art since 1933. It is on display in their gallery. But Trump claims he owns the o-iginal painting, which has been seen during TV interviews in Trump Tower.

TOP SECRET

PHISHING AND SPAM

Many people saw the growth of the Internet in the 1990s as a great benefit for the spread of knowledge. However, it also proved a great benefit to criminals.

Computer crime is usually known as cybercrime. It comes in different forms and affects businesses as well as individuals. Cybercrime includes threatening businesses by hacking into their computer networks to steal information or to prevent the system from operating until a ransom has been paid. Some attacks on businesses such as retailers or banks result in the theft of the financial details of many thousands of customers. Criminals also try to gain similar information directly from individual computer users. There are various ways to do this, such as by infecting a computer with software that records any keystrokes made by the user. These keyloggers try to identify strings of numbers that might be bank account numbers or PINs. Screenshot managers allow criminals to take a screenshot of what is on a PC screen. They are usually used to try to learn details of a user's bank account or credit cards.

CLASSIFIED

>> Online Danger Being connected online has created new types of criminal activity.

FAST FACTS

GONE PHISHING!

Phishing is the deliberate attempt to lure people into providing sensitive information such as bank details and passwords. Individuals or gangs use fake websites and emails to steal the information, which they then use to steal money or create online accounts.

>> **Cyber Café** Users got online access for the price of a cup of coffee and a small fee.

WILD WEST

The early years of the Internet in the 1990s were like the Wild West. Everything was new, there was little control, and people were pioneering computer use. Cyber cafés were popular before home computers became affordable. People who used them often failed to delete their log-in details. Hackers stole the details and used them to create fake accounts or steal from bank accounts.

TOP SECRET

PHISHING HITS THE BIG TIME

The most common way in which cyber criminals try to learn personal data is through phishing (the name reflects the fact that criminals are fishing for information). Current phishing scams try to trick people into revealing their security information, usually by convincing them that they are dealing with a genuine organization, such as a bank.

Phishing began in the early years of the Internet, when it took other forms. One common phishing scam began in Nigeria. Someone would send an email claiming to have been robbed while overseas. They wrote (often in poor English) a message asking for money to help them. The email pretended to be from a friend of the target of the scam, and it asked the target to send money as quickly as possible.

It took criminals a while to figure out better ways to steal online. It made it easier that, at the time, most people used the same provider, America Online (AOL). Phishers stole passwords and used **algorithms** to create millions of credit card numbers.

>> Lagos, Nigeria In the early days of the Internet, Nigeria was the source of many phishing emails.

The phishers used computers to match the stolen passwords to random credit card numbers. Every now and then, the two corresponded, and the phishers used the details to open new AOL accounts and access victims' bank accounts. In 1995, AOL introduced security measures that halted the use of randomly generated credit card numbers. Phishers switched to emailing customers pretending to be AOL employees and asking them to update their security information. Few people at the time were aware of the security problems of the Internet, so many handed over their details.

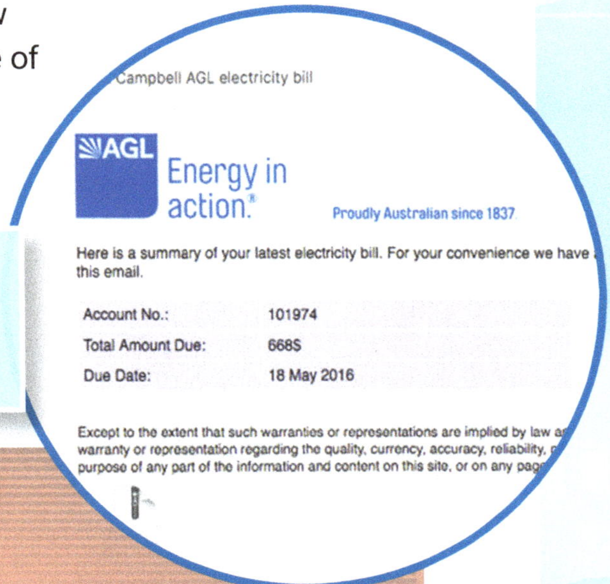

>> Spoof website
Many phishing websites resemble those of banks or utility companies.

WHAT DO YOU THINK?

Phishing websites try to copy the original exactly. They try to get users to click on pop-up menus, rather than entering website addresses in the address bar. Clicking on a pop-up or email link takes the user to fake sites. Given that most people know criminals are operating online, should individual computer users be responsible for protecting their own data?

>> Internet Banking Any time you log in to an online account, it is technically possible for hackers to steal your details.

PHISHING SCAMS

In the early 2000s, phishers targeted online commerce. They registered websites that resembled online businesses such as eBay and PayPal. Then they sent millions of emails that led customers to these sites, asking them to update their security information. The sites were similar enough to the genuine sites for people to be tricked. Modern phishing follows a similar process, but it more often involves fake bank checking accounts. After creating websites that look identical to those of real banks, criminals use emails to try to get customers to log on to the fake account. The fake site has a pop-up box that will only go off screen when the customer enters a card and PIN. The criminals use the details to access their checking accounts and steal their money.

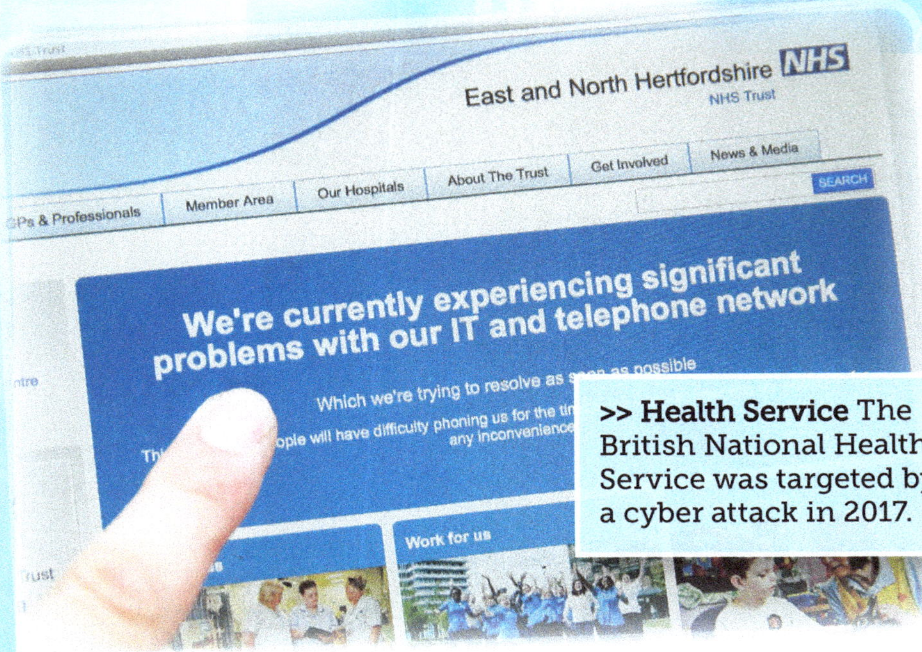

>> Health Service The British National Health Service was targeted by a cyber attack in 2017.

MALWARE AND RANSOMWARE

Some phishing scams place malware on a victim's computer, for example to log keystrokes. Some criminal gangs are now using sophisticated malware to target large organizations. They hack into computer systems with ransomware to disable the system until a ransom is paid. Once inside a system, the ransomeware spreads rapidly between linked users. In 2017, criminals targeted Great Britain's National Health Service as part of a global cyber attack that affected 300,000 computers and also hit delivery firm FedEx. In Britain, hospitals and doctors had to turn patients away. The criminals demanded a ransom paid in bitcoins. Bitcoin is a cybercurrency that exists only online. Some critics say that Bitcoin, which is difficult to trace, makes it easier for cyber criminals to get away with ransom money.

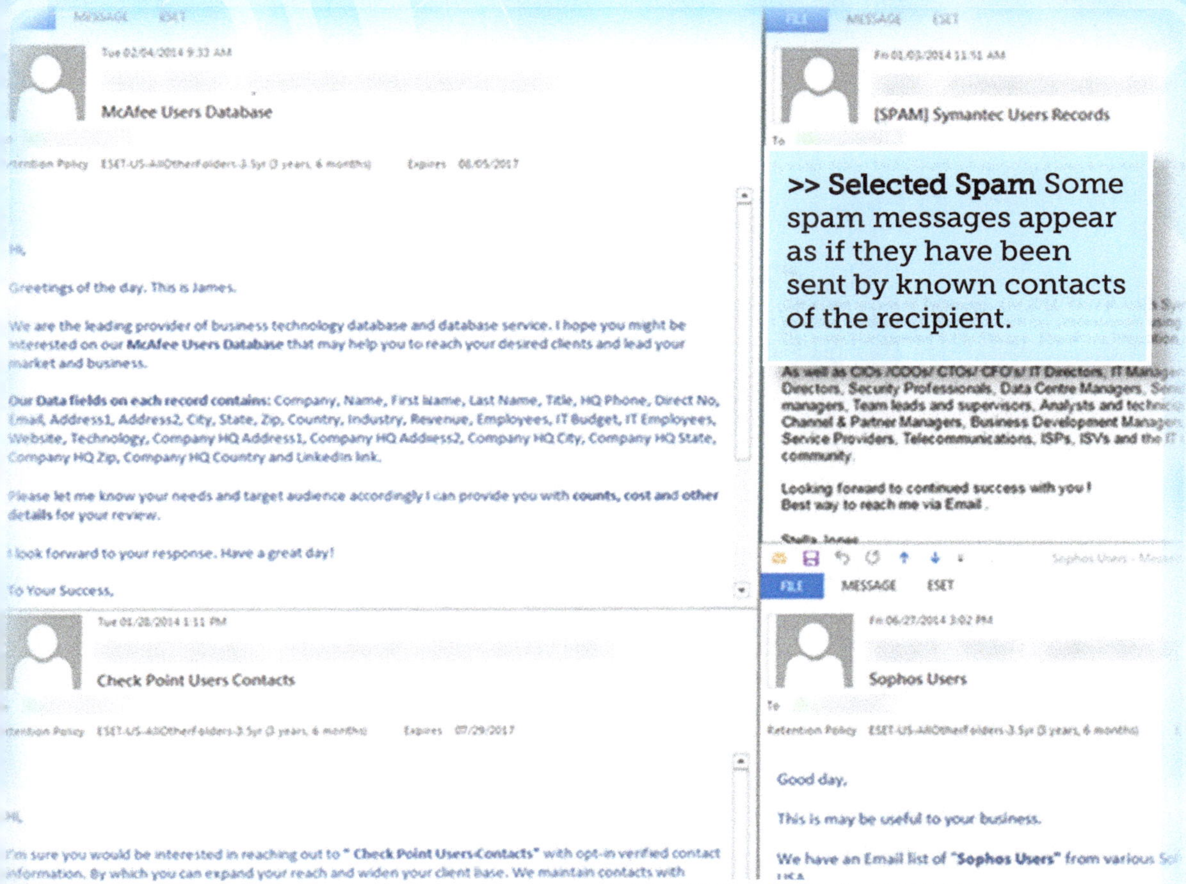

>> **Selected Spam** Some spam messages appear as if they have been sent by known contacts of the recipient.

FOR AND AGAINST

More than 100 billion spam emails are sent every day. Spam is junk emails that are sent without the permission of the recipient. Some try to sell things, but others contain links to malware. People who generate spam say it is a legitimate service that takes advantage of the popularity of the Internet to offer services. Many people argue that sending spam emails should be seen as a crime, because the main intention is to defraud people.

ILLEGAL DRUGS

One of the most profitable illegal trades is drugs. It is second only to illegal counterfeiting in revenue and is worth between $425 and $650 billion annually.

In the United States, users spend about $100 billion a year on illegal drugs. The drugs range from marijuana, which is legal in some states, to cocaine and heroin. Heroin belongs to a class of drugs called opioids, which also includes some prescription painkillers. In the last few years, opioid use has become a major problem in some parts of the United States.

The U.S. government spends around $50 billion a year fighting the illegal drug trade. The effort is led by the Drug Enforcement Administration (DEA) in the United States and the Central Intelligence Agency (CIA) in countries where drugs originate. Most drugs are imported to the United States from South and Central America through Mexico. The drug trade is controlled by associations of manufacturers known as **cartels**. The cartels have a long record of using violence and corruption. More recently, they have begun using technology to help them move their drugs around.

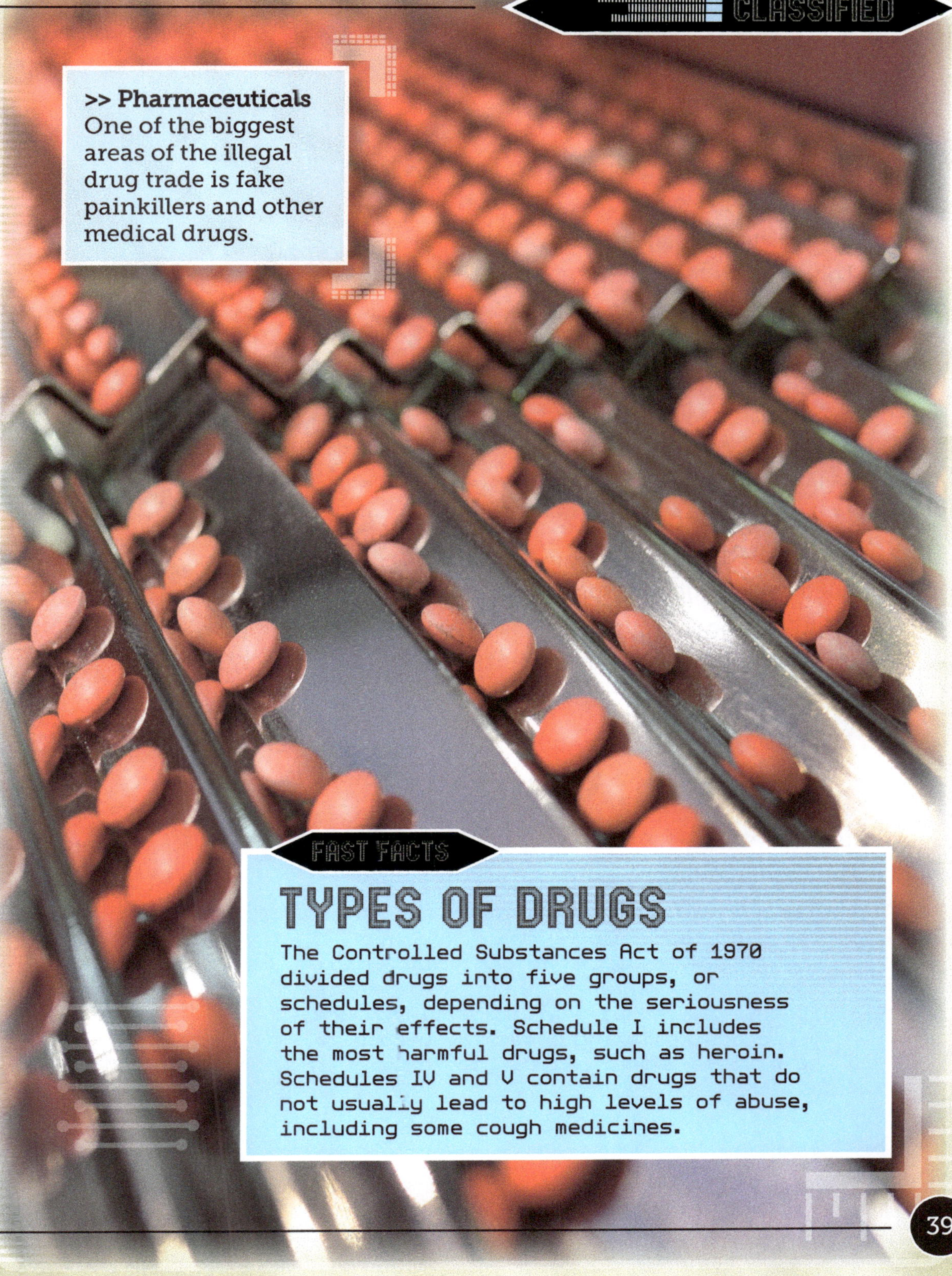

>> Pharmaceuticals
One of the biggest areas of the illegal drug trade is fake painkillers and other medical drugs.

FAST FACTS

TYPES OF DRUGS

The Controlled Substances Act of 1970 divided drugs into five groups, or schedules, depending on the seriousness of their effects. Schedule I includes the most harmful drugs, such as heroin. Schedules IV and V contain drugs that do not usually lead to high levels of abuse, including some cough medicines.

MAKING MONEY

The potential profits that can be made from drug smuggling are huge. This attracts thousands of people. The business begins with farmers who are paid more by cartels to grow drugs than they could earn growing other crops. In Colombia, farmers grow coca leaves used to make cocaine. In Afghanistan, farmers grow poppies that are used to make heroin.

>> Colombia Farmer
A farmer spreads out coca leaves to dry in the sunlight after the harvest.

WHAT DO YOU THINK?

The question of whether drugs should be legalized has occupied governments for decades. While drugs remain illegal, dealers make huge profits but pay no taxes on them. Making the trade legal might make it easier to control. For many people, however, drugs are a **moral** issue. They argue that legalizing drugs would be legalizing a way for people to harm themselves. What do you think?

Drug cartels hire local farmworkers and fishermen to process and transport the crops. The workers earn more money than they would in legal occupations. However, the drug cartels do not only operate by offering rewards. They also use threats and violence to force people to cooperate with them.

TRADE IN COLOMBIA

Colombia in South America is the world's leading producer of cocaine. Cocaine is made from the leaves of the native coca plant, which grows in Colombia. **Indigenous** people chew the leaves to help with **altitude sickness**. The main market for cocaine is the United States and Western Europe.

>> **Arrested** Members of a Mexican drug gang are lined up by the police together with the weapons they had when arrested.

>> U.S. Crisis
Marchers protest the growth in deaths related to opioids such as heroin in the United States.

Drugs are trafficked mainly by land and sea from Colombia through Central America and Mexico into the United States. Today's traffickers are using **drones** to transport drugs. In January 2015, a drone crashed on the US border with Mexico. It was loaded with crystal meth. This is a manufactured drug that can be made cheaply and sold at a high price.

Along with drones, drug traffickers use more established technology. They use a **global positioning system (GPS)** to try to avoid attempts to intercept drug shipments. Rather than shipping cocaine on boats, they wrap packages in floating waterproof packets together with a GPS tracker. They drop the packages in the sea so that ocean currents will take them near the coast of North America, where they can be tracked and retrieved. With lots of packages in the sea it is hard for the U.S. drug enforcement patrols to find them all.

LEGAL CANNABIS

In 2014, the sale of cannabis or marijuana (below) became legal in Colorado. In the first 10 months of 2016 alone, the trade raised $150 million in taxes on sales of $1 billion. However, federal law prohibits banks and credit-card companies from taking drug money. Legal marijuana stores can only sell drugs for cash. They have so much cash in their stores they have to hire their own high-level security in order to protect their stores.

TOP SECRET

THE CRIMINALS

Many people involved in the drugs trade make limited amounts of money. However, those who control the supply of drugs at the top of the chain can make fortunes. During the early 1990s, the Colombian Pablo Escobar controlled around 80 percent of the world's cocaine supply. His motto was "plato o plomo," which roughly translates as "money or a bullet." In practice, that meant that he used his power and money to try to bribe officials. But if they refused to cooperate, he had them killed. Escobar was richer than the Colombian state. His personal fortune was worth around $50 billion in today's money.

>> Drug Kingpin
Pablo Escobar was shot and killed by Colombian police in 1993.

FOR AND AGAINST

When Pablo Escobar ran the Colombian drug cartel, he used some of the profits from his drug empire to help local people. He built schools, churches, and hospitals around Medellin, where he lived. He built houses so that everyone had a roof over their head and he set up soccer schools and leagues across the country. As a result, many Colombians saw him as a hero. However, many others saw him as a criminal who made Medellin the murder capital of the world.

STOPPING DRUGS

The agencies tasked with stopping the drugs trade rely on various methods. They gather information from informers, for example. However, they are also using modern technology. Satellite photographs and **surveillance** drones allow them to identify places where drugs are being grown or processed. Law enforcement agencies have their own computer experts who hack into drug dealers' accounts to discover where they keep their money. Such efforts face a constant challenge from criminals whose operations are constantly becoming more sophisticated. As in other areas of crime, the fight for law and order is increasingly fought through a combination of traditional detective work and the latest technology.

>> **Seized** U.S. Coast Guards with a shipment of cocaine intercepted on its way to the United States.

GLOSSARY

algorithms Sets of rules followed by a computer to solve problems.

altitude sickness An illness caused by shortage of oxygen at high levels.

anonymity The condition of not revealing one's name or identity.

assets Property, money, and other valuable belongings of a person or group.

blackmailing Demanding money in return for not revealing damaging information.

blind trust A body that runs the businesses of a person in public office.

bribing Giving people gifts or money to persuade them to do something illegal.

capitalism An economic system based on private businesses.

cartels Associations that cooperate to keep prices high and restrict competition.

corrupt Willing to act dishonestly in return for personal gain.

counterfeiters People who make exact copies of something valuable.

cybercrime Criminal activity carried out using computers or the Internet.

Dark Web Part of the Internet that is only accessible using special software, where users are able to remain anonymous.

drones Unmanned aerial vehicles that are usually flown by remote control.

fraud Criminal deception in order to make money.

global positioning system (GPS) A system that uses satellites to pinpoint locations on Earth.

hackers People who gain unauthorized access to computer systems.

identity theft Using another person's name and details to gain credit or purchase goods.

illicit Forbidden by the law.

indigenous Describes the original people who lived in a region.

life expectancy The average length of time a person is expected to live.

loyalty Faithfully supporting a person or idea.

malware Software intended to damage or disrupt a computer.

moral Relating to questions of good or bad behavior.

naivety A lack of wisdom or judgment.

notorious Famous because of bad deeds.

offshore Describes businesses registered in locations with low taxes.

private sector The part of the economy owned by private individuals.

ransom A sum of money paid in return for the release or return of something.

satellite An artificial spacecraft in orbit around Earth.

surveillance The careful watching of a place or an individual, such as a suspected criminal.

trafficking Dealing in something illegal.

viruses Malware that spreads from computer to computer.

FURTHER RESOURCES

Books

Harmon, Daniel E. *Cyber Attacks, Counterattacks, and Espionage*. Cryptography: Code Making and Code Breaking. New York: Rosen Young Adult, 2017.

Haugen, David. *Organized Crime*. Opposing Viewpoints. Detroit: Greenhaven Press, 2014.

Somerville, Clive. *The Drug Enforcement Administration*. Defending Our Nation. Broomall, PA: Mason Crest, 2017.

Wood, Alix. *Hunting the Cyber Trail: Be a Computer Forensic Scientist*. Crime Solvers. New York: Gareth Stevens, 2017.

Websites

Computer Hacking
computer.howstuffworks.com/hacker.htm
How Stuff Works explains how computer hackers operate.

Drug Trafficking
www.unodc.org/unodc/en/drug-trafficking/index.html
This United Nations page is an introduction to the global drug trade.

Identity Theft
money.howstuffworks.com/identity-theft.htm
This article from How Stuff Works explains how criminals steal identities and use them.

The Mafia
www.history.com/topics/mafia-in-the-united-states
A history of the Mafia crime organization in the United States.

Publisher's note to educators and parents: Our editors have carefully reviewed these websites to ensure that they are suitable for students. Many websites change frequently, however, and we cannot guarantee that a site's future contents will continue to meet our high standards of quality and educational value. Be advised that students should be closely supervised whenever they access the Internet.

INDEX